The Changing Role of Women

Mandy Ross

Heinemann Library
Chicago, Illinois

© 2002 Reed Educational & Professional Publishing
Published by Heinemann Library,
an imprint of Reed Educational & Professional Publishing,
Chicago, Illinois

Customer Service 888-454-2279

Visit our website at www.heinemannlibrary.com

Produced for Heinemann Library by Discovery Books Limited
Designed by Ian Winton
Consultant: Kate Nash
Originated by Dot Gradations
Printed in China by Wing King Tong

08 07 06
10 9 8 7 6 5 4 3 2

Library of Congress Cataloging-in-Publication...
Ross, Mandy.
  The changing role of women / Mandy Ross.
    p. cm. -- (20th-century perspectives)
Includes bibliographical references and index.
Summary: Examines the changing role of women throughout the twentieth
century in the areas of politics, human rights, education, domestic
life, work, health care, the arts, fashion, and sports.
  ISBN 1-58810-660-8 (lib. bdg.)   ISBN 1-58810-920-8 (pbk. bdg.)
  1. Women--History--Juvenile literature. 2. Sex
role--History--Juvenile literature. [1. Women--History. 2. Sex
role--History.] I. Title. II. Series.
  HQ1121 .R67 2002
  305.42'09--dc21

                                2001004813

Acknowledgments
The author and publishers are grateful to the following for permission to reproduce copyright material: p. 4 Lewes W. Hine/Hulton Archive Photos; pp. 5, 29, 31 Peter Newark's American Pictures; pp. 6, 33 Hulton Deutsch Collection; pp. 7, 8, 9 Peter Newark's Historical Pictures; pp. 10, 14, 15, 17, 32, 34, 36, 39 Jacques Demarthon/Popperfoto; pp. 11, 18, 25, 38 Hulton Getty; pp. 12, 22, 24, 27, 28 Bettmann/Corbis; pp. 13, 30 Huton Deutsch Collection/Corbis; p. 16 Peter Turnley/Corbis; p. 19 Liba Taylor/Corbis; p. 20 Humphrey Spender/Hulton Archive Photos; p. 21 David Rubinger/Corbis; p. 23 Earl and Nazima Kowall/Corbis; pp. 26, 41, 43 Reuters/Popperfoto; p. 35 Marc Garanger/Corbis; p. 37 Redferns; p. 40 Ann Hawthorn/Corbis; p. 42 Zed Nelson/Panos Pictures.

Cover photograph reproduced with permission of Hulton Deutsch Collection/Corbis.

Special thanks to Nesta Ross, Myra Connell, and Karen Whiteside.

Every effort has been made to contact copyright holders of any material reproduced in this book. Any omissions will be rectified in subsequent printings if notice is given to the publisher.

Some words are shown in bold, **like this.** You can find out what they mean by looking in the glossary.

Contents

Women in 1900

It might be hard for women in the **developed** world today to imagine how different women's lives were in the **West** only a hundred years ago—and how different they still are in many parts of the world. In 1900, most women's lives were spent at the bidding of men. Women were not free to control their lives, their property, or even their own bodies. They were not treated as full adults, but like inferior humans who could not be trusted to make their own decisions.

Women's lives

Without **birth control,** women often had large families and would spend most of their lives pregnant and caring for children. In 1900, almost no women had the right to vote, so they had no right to question how their country was run. In many countries, women were under the control of their fathers or husbands, who also controlled any money or property they owned. Many women could not live **independently** because they could not earn a living.

Rich and poor

Wealthy women's lives were very different from poor women's lives. In 1900, women in rich families rarely went to work and lived a life of leisure and boredom, supported by their husbands. In working-class families, life for women was very hard. Women worked long hours, often in poor conditions, in factories or out in the fields. Yet despite their long working hours, these women were still expected to look after their homes and their children.

Few countries had any kind of **welfare system** in 1900. Families had to look after themselves, and if they could not earn enough money, they went hungry. Women with children whose husbands had died or left them were especially vulnerable.

These women immigrants and their children sew garments in a cramped New York apartment early in the twentieth century. Around the world, many women worked in dreadful conditions, often for very low wages.

Women in the colonies

In 1900, many countries in Africa and Asia were **colonies,** which means that they were ruled by other nations, such as Britain or France. The people there lived in poverty and were denied rights. They were excluded from education and well-paid jobs. Women were described as "slaves of slaves," under the control of their husbands or fathers, as well as the colonial power.

Call for women's rights

From the 1840s onward, many women in the Western world had begun to question the old ways. Two such women, Elizabeth Cady Stanton and Lucretia Mott, organized one of the first women's rights conferences in Seneca Falls, New York in 1848, to "discuss the social, civil, and religious conditions of women." Stanton joined Susan B. Anthony, another supporter of women's rights, in founding the National Woman **Suffrage** Association in 1869. These "new women," as they were called, wanted more rights and freedoms. They questioned old ideas about marriage and family life. **Feminists** (both men and women) believed that every woman should be independent and active, and should be treated equally with men. Women should make their own decisions and, most urgently of all, they should have the right to vote.

In some countries, women took up arms to fight for their beliefs. These women "soldaderas" fought against poverty and the power of the landowners during the Mexican revolution, which began in 1910.

Women's rights

"Women's rights" refers to women having the right to take their part in society, use their skills, and fulfill their potential. The struggle for women's rights is not only to achieve equal treatment for women and men, but to recognize the value of women and what they do, as well as to overcome barriers to equality at work and in politics. This battle is not over yet, and in some parts of the world women's lives are very far from equal.

Fighting for the Vote

At the start of the twentieth century, very few women around the world had **suffrage,** or the right to vote. Without this right, women's views and wishes could be completely ignored, even when governments made decisions affecting women's lives. Women who campaigned for the right to vote were called **suffragettes** or **suffragists.** Not all men had the right to vote either—often only rich and powerful men had this right. In addition, many countries were still ruled by unelected monarchs, emperors, or dictators. The struggle for suffrage was one of the key issues at the start of the twentieth century.

Campaigning in the United States

Members of the National Woman Suffrage Association held meetings, bonfires, and street dances, and they used new media such as the movies, advertising, and radio to build support for women's votes. But progress was disappointingly slow. Also, there was tension between the movements for African-American rights and women's suffrage, as some African Americans saw women's suffrage as a distraction from the battle for racial equality.

Shock tactics in Britain

Moderate suffragists participated in huge processions carrying banners and wearing sashes. Crowds of supporters gathered to watch and cheer them, creating a carnival-like atmosphere. At one procession in London in April 1909, marchers dressed in the clothes of their trades to show that women from all backgrounds were united in the suffrage movement: nurses in uniform, poultry farmers carrying baskets of eggs, women from mining communities in shawls, and many others. Famous actresses marched among them as well.

By 1908, impatient at their lack of progress, the more radical suffragettes in Britain turned to shock tactics. As well as organizing huge demonstrations, they chained themselves to railings, broke windows, and stormed government

Crowds of supporters lined the streets to watch a suffragette procession move through London in 1911.

buildings. Many deliberately got themselves arrested and sent to prison to publicize their cause. Some people, particularly the media, were outraged by these violent tactics and thought they did nothing to further the women's cause.

In prison, some suffragettes went on hunger strikes and were fed by force, using tubes pushed down their throats. Some were released when they grew weak, only to be re-imprisoned when they had regained their strength. The suffragettes' courage won them widespread admiration among men and women of all backgrounds.

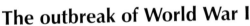

Japanese women in Tokyo call for the right to vote in 1929. Women did not gain the right to vote in Japan until 1945.

The outbreak of World War I

The campaigners for women's suffrage put their cause on hold when World War I broke out in 1914. They instead turned their energy to war work. In many countries, this, probably more than anything else, helped women achieve the right to vote, although women in some European countries had to wait until after World War II.

Women's suffrage around the world

Women's suffrage was not just a **Western** movement. In 1918, the Women's Indian Association persuaded the newly-formed Indian National Congress to support women's right to vote. In Japan, the Seithoscha **feminist** group called for suffrage and other rights for women. Meanwhile in China, the Chinese Suffragette Society demanded political and voting rights for women, and an end to the tradition of footbinding (where girls' feet were broken and bound to make them very small). The Egyptian Feminist Union, created in 1923, called for women's votes, health care, craft workshops for poor women, and child care centers for working mothers.

Mary Wollstonecraft

The struggle for women's rights started long before the twentieth century. An Englishwoman, Mary Wollstonecraft, was inspired by the 1789 French Revolution when she wrote *A Vindication of the Rights of Woman* in 1792, in which she argued for educational and social rights for women.

Women in Politics 1914–1945

World War I (1914–18) changed people's attitudes toward women. All around the world, women served their country by taking over the work done by the men who had gone off to fight. They proved women could work as hard and as skilfully as men. After the war, women's demand for the vote, once so controversial, seemed much less outrageous. In country after country, women gained the right to vote. And new nations such as Austria, Czechoslovakia, and Poland, established in 1918–19 from the break-up of old empires, introduced women's **suffrage** from the start.

The Hague peace convention

In 1915, over one thousand women peace campaigners from twelve countries met in the Dutch capital, The Hague. They called for an end to war and for women's right to vote. The Women's International League for Peace and Freedom was formed at The Hague, and still exists today.

The Russian Revolution brought many changes in women's lives, sometimes for the better. This poster tells women that while they go to work in the Soviet factories, their children will be well cared for in state nurseries.

Women voters and politicians

In Britain, women over the age of 30 were granted the right to vote in 1918 (although it was not until ten years later that all women could vote from the age of 21, the same age as men). Women in the United States finally got the right to vote in 1920. Once they could vote, women started to run for political positions in elections. Ironically, many early women in government were not great supporters of women's rights. Other women in government did try to improve the lives of women, but struggled in the male-dominated field of politics.

New freedom for women?

As well as the right to vote, the 1920s brought new freedoms and excitement for women such as movies, jazz music, and dancing. Although there was a dazzling array of new consumer goods, such as refrigerators and vacuum cleaners, only the wealthy could afford them for their servants to use. Working-class women did not benefit from such labor-saving devices for several decades.

Women could vote, but because there were very few women active in government, little progress was made in terms of women's rights. Some of the opportunities women experienced during the war years were soon lost. In Britain, for example, the Marriage Bar banned married women from working in civil service, local government, and many other fields. The Marriage Bar was only dismantled during World War II.

A woman works in a munitions factory during World War I. Women's war work helped earn them the right to vote in many countries when the war came to an end.

Women and the Russian Revolution

World War I caused terrible hardship in Russia. In 1917, weary of the long lines for rationed bread, the women of Petrograd rioted against food shortages and the loss of life in the war. Men joined the women's riots, which grew and spread until they became a **revolution,** toppling Tsar Nicholas II, and eventually creating a new **Communist** nation, the Soviet Union.

Soviet women gained the right to vote in 1917, although this right allowed them to vote for only one party in the new system of government. Millions of women learned to read and write in a vast **literacy** campaign. They worked alongside men in heavy industry and construction projects to build their new nation.

WOMEN'S SUFFRAGE

THIS TABLE SHOWS THE SPREAD OF WOMEN'S SUFFRAGE AROUND THE WORLD. ALTHOUGH WOMEN IN MANY COUNTRIES GAINED THE RIGHT TO VOTE AFTER WORLD WAR I, SOME EUROPEAN COUNTRIES, SUCH AS FRANCE AND ITALY, HELD BACK UNTIL AFTER WORLD WAR II.

1893 NEW ZEALAND	1934 BRAZIL
1902* AUSTRALIA	1937 PHILIPPINES
1906 FINLAND	1944 JAMAICA
1913 NORWAY	1945 FRANCE
1915 DENMARK	1945 ITALY
1917 SOVIET UNION	1945 JAPAN
1918** BRITAIN	1949 CHINA
1918 GERMANY	1949 INDIA
1918 NETHERLANDS	1952 MEXICO
1920 CANADA	1956 EGYPT
1920 UNITED STATES	1964 KENYA
1932 CEYLON (NOW	1971 SWITZERLAND
SRI LANKA)	1982 JORDAN

* ABORIGINAL WOMEN AND MEN ONLY GAINED THE RIGHT TO VOTE IN 1967.
** BRITAIN GRANTED THE VOTE IN 1918 TO WOMEN AGED 30 AND OVER AND TO ALL WOMEN IN 1928.

Eleanor Roosevelt 1884-1962

Eleanor Roosevelt, wife of President Franklin Roosevelt, used her position as First Lady to campaign for the rights of women and African-Americans. She campaigned to improve workers' rights, and worked to persuade the **United Nations** to adopt the Universal Declaration of Human Rights in 1948.

Women in Politics from 1945

During World War II (1939–45) women were once again enlisted to work in the fields and factories of the warring nations of the world, replacing the men who were called to fight. The years after World War II brought huge changes around the world. Governments adjusted to peace and growing wealth by setting up **welfare systems.** Many countries in Africa and Asia fought for **independence** from European rule, and gradually a few women were elected as political leaders.

Post-war welfare systems

As economies grew stronger again, many **Western** governments set up welfare policies to make sure that everyone had enough money to live on, as well as health care and education. Women benefited from these policies; for instance, in Britain, child benefit, a weekly allowance paid by the government to help with the cost of raising a family, was paid directly to the mother. Many women worked in the new welfare systems, too, as teachers, nurses, and social workers.

After the assassination of her husband in 1959, Mrs. Sirimavo Bandaranaike was elected prime minister of Sri Lanka. This made her the first woman to be elected as a national leader.

Women in the fight for independence

After World War II, many **colonies** began to fight for their independence, and women played their part in these struggles. In India, women **boycotted** shops selling foreign goods, spoke at rallies, and led demonstrations that helped bring about the country's independence in 1948. In Algeria, women fought alongside men in the long struggle to overthrow French rule, and finally succeeded in 1962. But Algerian women were disappointed when their lives did not change a great deal after independence.

High fliers: women as political leaders

Since the 1960s, individual women have risen to great heights in politics. Mrs. Sirimavo Bandaranaike was the first woman to be elected as a national leader

Algerian women's liberation?

We are the daughters of those women who waged a liberation war and whose only liberation was to return to their kitchen.

Fatma Oussedik, Algerian sociologist, 1984

when she became the prime minister of Sri Lanka in 1960. She was followed in 1966 by Indira Gandhi in India and Golda Meir in Israel in 1969.

In the West, Margaret Thatcher was Britain's first woman prime minister, and held the position from 1979 to 1990. In the United States in 1997, Madeleine Albright became secretary of state. She was the first woman to hold this position and the highest-ranking woman in the history of the U.S. government.

Not all women leaders are champions of women's rights. British prime minister Margaret Thatcher presided over an all-male cabinet and her government's welfare cuts, especially in maternity benefits, hit some women hard.

Getting more women into government

Most traditional political parties are male-dominated and have more men than women among their members. This means that fewer women run as candidates for election to government. Today, the average figure around the world for women in government is only 12.7 percent. In the United States, the percentage of women serving in Congress is around 14 percent. Scandinavian countries have the best record for the number of women in government—around 40 percent of their elected politicians are women.

Political parties in some countries have taken positive action to encourage more women to enter the field of politics. In Britain, the Labour party is trying to cut parliament's long working hours to help women politicians balance their work lives with their families' needs.

International action for women

The **United Nations (UN)** encourages individual governments around the world to work to improve human rights. With women's rights specifically in mind, the UN has set up projects with the aim of empowering women—that is, giving women the tools and skills they need to improve their own lives, rather than waiting for government action. One example is a plan that loans women in developing countries small amounts of money to start their own businesses. This builds women's confidence, and also raises their status within their communities.

Women in Civil Rights Movements

The struggle for racial equality and **civil rights** was a major issue in the twentieth century. Women have played an important role in this struggle, although sometimes they have had to stand up for women's rights within these movements. Many have linked the struggle for civil rights with that of women's rights. Great progress has been made, but racism and ethnic hatred are still problems in many parts of the world.

Elizabeth Eckford enters Little Rock High School surrounded by protestors and armed guards in September 1957. This attempt at integrating African Americans into the white school system had to be ordered and enforced by the U.S. Federal Court.

Women in the American civil rights movement

In December 1955, an African-American woman, Rosa Parks, was arrested for refusing to give up her seat on a bus to a white man. Her arrest sparked the American civil rights movement, which campaigned for equal rights for African Americans. Supporters sometimes met with violence from angry whites, but by 1965, **segregation** was banned by law, although some states in the deep South, such as Mississippi and Arkansas, resisted the changes for years.

Risking violence

Supporting the civil rights movement was dangerous. One African-American woman remembers deciding to take that risk, since it seemed that whites had been trying to kill her *"a little bit at a time ever since I could remember."*

In South Africa

Meanwhile, women in South Africa joined the fight against **apartheid** alongside their men. In 1956, a 20,000-person-strong march protested laws that restricted black men and women's freedom to travel, and violated other rights as well. Under the apartheid system, black and mixed-race children received only basic education. In the 1950s, school **boycotts** were organized in protest. Women set up informal schools so that black children would not miss out on their education.

Woman also played their part in the political struggle against apartheid. Winnie Mandela was an executive of the ANC (African National Congress) Women's League. After it was banned, many of its women leaders worked within the Federation of South African Women.

Apartheid was finally abolished in 1994, when democratic elections were held in South Africa and Nelson Mandela was elected president. Now more than a quarter of South African members of Parliament are women, and the government has worked hard to improve women's rights, health care, and employment conditions.

In Cato Manor near Durban, South Africa, black women riot in protest at government measures to "clean up" their township in June 1959. The townships where black workers and their families lived were separated from the towns where whites lived.

Indigenous people's rights

In North and South America, Australia, and New Zealand, **indigenous people** (the original inhabitants) were thrown off their land when white settlers arrived. By the twentieth century, most lived in poverty with no citizenship rights at all. In some Latin American countries, such as Guatemala, government troops attacked, tortured, and sometimes murdered indigenous people. Indigenous women have campaigned for their people's rights to land, their culture, and citizenship. In 1992, Rigoberta Menchú, a Guatemalan Mayan woman, was awarded the Nobel Peace Prize for her work defending indigenous people's rights.

In Australia until the 1960s, many Aboriginal children were taken away from their mothers without consent, to be raised in white families. This was an attempt to destroy Aboriginal culture and language. Across Australia, millions of women of all races and backgrounds joined organizations supporting Aboriginal rights.

Women's Activism

Many women have rejected the goals of male leaders and oppressive governments. They were concerned instead with **human rights** and environmental issues. All around the world, women have taken action to make their views heard, often using imaginative and daring tactics to get their message across.

The "Mothers of the Disappeared" in Argentina

In the 1970s, a brutal military government ruled Argentina. Up to 20,000 people were kidnapped by soldiers and never seen again. Evidence eventually emerged showing that most had been tortured and then murdered. These people became known as the "disappeared." Braving great danger, the "Mothers of the Disappeared" protested against the murders by walking silently around the central square of Buenos Aires, wearing white head scarves and carrying photographs of their children.

"Mothers of the Disappeared" weep during a protest against the torture and murder of thousands of people by the Argentine military government during the 1970s.

Women and the environment

Women have found peaceful methods of holding demonstrations on environmental issues, too. Often, especially in **developing countries,** women grow the food for their families, and so are particularly concerned about damage to the environment. In Uttar Pradesh in northern India, forest **felling** by commercial companies was causing frequent floods and landslides. Homes and livelihoods were threatened. In 1973, local women decided to organize protests to prevent any more trees from being cut down. They marched into the forest and hugged the trees, protecting them with their own bodies to stop the felling.

Women for peace

Another movement in which women played an important role was the anti-nuclear campaign of the 1980s. Hundreds of

Trees and human rights

Professor Wangari Mathaai, a Kenyan woman, is the founder of the environmental Green Belt Movement. Under her leadership, 50,000 women and school children planted more than ten million trees in Kenya, improving the land and preventing soil erosion. In 1992, she was arrested and beaten for supporting human rights.

thousands of women in North America and Europe protested against the build-up of nuclear weapons. They rejected their governments' military strategy of nuclear deterrence, which means that each **superpower** stockpiles enough nuclear weapons to destroy each other several times over to deter the other side from starting a war. Many protesters were women who had never been in demonstrations before, but who wanted to raise their families in peace, without fear of nuclear war.

Women set up peace camps outside army and nuclear weapons bases in Europe, Australia, and North America. Eventually, many weapons were dismantled or removed from Europe as **Cold War** tensions eased after the late 1980s.

Women across the divide

Some longstanding conflicts, such as those in Northern Ireland and the Middle East, have affected women and their families for many generations. Yet despite the fear, violence, and hatred that often characterize such conflicts, women have succeeded in working together to promote peace. They often focus on interests common to women from any background, rather than on the religious or political differences that divide them. Some of these common issues are **domestic violence**, rape, child care, and working conditions.

In 1997, Protestant and Catholic women formed the Women's Coalition in Northern Ireland, helping to bridge the gap between the main parties in peace talks. Here, a woman holds a paper dove at a Belfast peace rally.

Guns or health care?

In 1986, Swedish anti-militarist campaigner Inga Thorsson compared health and military spending around the world: *There is one soldier per 43 people, but only one doctor for 1,030 people. Every minute 30 children die from hunger and disease, but every minute the world spends $2 million for military purposes.*

In 1997, Protestant and Catholic women formed the Women's Coalition in Northern Ireland. At the peace talks of 1997–98 they helped bridge gaps between the main parties. In Israel, a movement called Coalition of Women for a Just Peace brings together Israeli and Palestinian women. They work to break down barriers between the two cultures, and to try and create a fair and lasting peace.

Women and Human Rights

Every man, woman, and child has **human rights.** This means they have the right to live without fear for their life or freedom. Human rights began to be defined after 1945, but statements and declarations of human rights are not always properly enforced, and there are many violations around the world. Violations of women's human rights are often specifically related to their sex.

What are human rights?

In response to terrible abuses during World War II, human rights were set out in the **United Nations'** Universal Declaration of Human Rights in 1948. This charter, signed by governments all around the world, defines freedoms to which every human being is entitled, whatever their sex, race, language, or religion. These freedoms include the right to a fair trial and not to be tortured or unfairly imprisoned, the rights to privacy, marriage, family life, political rights, and equality.

Women as refugees

Refugees are people who have been forced to flee their homes to escape violence and persecution. Often they are escaping from human rights violations, and they may be vulnerable to further violations as they seek a safe place to stay. Women and children make up more than half of the world's estimated twelve million refugees. Women are sometimes escaping persecution solely because of their sex, for instance, to escape a forced marriage, and have often struggled to be accepted as refugees.

Women refugees, like these Kurdish women, must often rely on help from other nations to feed and clothe their families because they are unable to work or grow food as they could in their homeland.

Rape as a war crime

In wars throughout history, soldiers have raped women of the opposing side. A terrible example of this was the organized campaign of rape of Bosnian women by Serb soldiers during the war in the former Yugoslavia in the 1990s. Eventually, some of the soldiers who had taken part were prosecuted and imprisoned by an international court for human rights violations. This was the first time that rape had been successfully prosecuted as a war crime.

Contemporary slavery

Slavery was abolished in most countries in the nineteenth century, but new forms of slavery capture many thousands of girls and women around the world, denying them their human rights. Child labor is one form, with hundreds of thousands of girls and boys forced to work instead of going to school; for instance, in West Africa, harvesting the cocoa crops sold to make chocolate, or in parts of Asia making shoes for **multinational corporations.** In some Asian countries, many women and young girls are trapped by poverty in domestic slavery, or in prostitution, where many have contracted HIV, the virus that leads to AIDS.

Double discrimination

Women with disabilities, like women in other minority groups, may experience double **discrimination.** Girls and women with disabilities face discrimination because of their disability as well as their gender. In societies where girls receive less schooling than boys, girls with disabilities may find it even harder to get an education. Around the world, women and men with disabilities are organizing campaigns for equal rights.

Aung San Suu Kyi

In 1990, Aung San Suu Kyi led her party to victory in elections in Burma (now Myanmar), ruled since 1962 by harsh military dictators. Despite this, she has not been allowed to govern, and was placed under **house arrest** until 1995. Even now her movements are limited to a small area. Each week, people gather outside her home, risking imprisonment to hear her speak. Her experience shows how human rights can be violated despite the UN Declaration of Human Rights and other international agreements, when they are not properly enforced.

Aung San Suu Kyi, was democratically elected the leader of Burma in 1990. Despite international protests, the military dictatorship has violated her human rights, keeping her under house arrest and refusing to allow her to govern.

Education of Girls and Women

Throughout the twentieth century, access to education came to be recognized as a basic **human right.** In 1958, the **United Nations** introduced its Convention against **Discrimination** in Education. Great improvements have been made in girls' and women's education in many countries, but there are still parts of the world where girls receive little or no schooling.

Educating wives and homemakers

Early in the twentieth century, the common belief was that education was wasted on girls, since they were destined only to become wives and mothers. As a result, girls, and especially girls from working-class families, were given only basic education, concentrating on homemaking skills such as cooking and sewing. Girls were not taught skills that would allow them to earn their own living and build a career.

Richer families could afford to pay for better schooling, although the curriculum offered to these girls was often weak on science and mathematics. This meant that girls who did go on to college were already steered toward arts subjects.

Women look on during a class at Women's College Hospital in Philadelphia in 1911. Around the world, women fought for many decades for the right to enter professions such as medicine.

Chinese women's education

In 1924, the Chinese women's movement issued this proclamation:
Let boys and girls receive the same instruction. Let all careers be open to girls. . . . Let the old educational system which produced "good wives and tender mothers" be abolished and one created which turns girls into real human beings.

Women and higher education

For centuries, women were not allowed to study at universities. This meant that many careers and professions were closed to them. When women students were allowed to study at universities and other institutions of higher education, they braved hostility and ridicule from male teachers and students.

THIS TABLE SHOWS WHEN WOMEN WERE FIRST ALLOWED TO STUDY AT UNIVERSITIES OR OTHER HIGHER EDUCATION INSTITUTIONS IN SOME COUNTRIES.

1833	UNITED STATES	1908	GERMANY
1871	BRITAIN	1915	TURKEY
1871	NETHERLANDS	1925	ISRAEL
1877	INDIA	1964	JORDAN
1882	NORWAY		

Maria Montessori

Maria Montessori (1870–1952) grew up in Italy. After training as a doctor, she opened a school for children with learning difficulties. Unhappy with existing teaching methods, she devised her own. She believed that young children learned best through play, taking responsibility for their own learning. These methods were also found to work with children without learning difficulties. Montessori's methods have influenced mainstream teaching methods all around the world.

Girls' and boys' grades

During the 1970s and 80s, there was concern in the **West** that girls were achieving lower grades than boys in traditionally male subjects, such as science and math. Teachers and educators worked hard to find ways of making these subjects more accessible to girls to build their confidence and improve their grades. Girls scores did improve, and in the last decade of the twentieth century, the tables began to turn. Boys' exam results slipped behind girls' in many subjects, even in some traditionally male ones. Now educators are looking at ways to bring boys' grades back up again to match girls' grades.

These women are learning to read in a Kenyan village. When women are educated, they go on to have fewer and healthier children—an important part of improving living conditions in developing countries.

Women and literacy

Despite real progress in tackling illiteracy over the last quarter of the twentieth century, by 2000 there were still an estimated 900 million illiterate adults, people who have never learned to read and write, around the world. Two-thirds of that number are women. Part of the reason for this is that in **developing countries** girls frequently receive less education than boys. Girls there are often expected to work at home or in the fields instead.

Research shows that in places where girls and women are well educated, the birth rate falls and they have fewer and healthier children. Encouraging families to send their daughters to school and improving women's **literacy** are two essential strategies for improving life in many developing countries.

Domestic Life

At the beginning of the twentieth century, women were mainly responsible for child care, as well as household tasks such as cooking, cleaning, and laundry. During the century, new machines such as refrigerators, vacuum cleaners, and washing machines transformed many of these tasks. But recent research shows that even today, women still do most of the housework.

Men's work, women's work

Men are traditionally seen as the breadwinners, bringing in money by working at a paid job outside the home. In contrast, women's work in the home remains unpaid and rarely acknowledged. And yet, without this unpaid domestic work, the economy would grind to a halt; on normal earnings, most men could not afford to pay a housekeeper, cook, and nanny to replace the work done by their wives.

Heavy labor at home

In the **West** in 1900, without electricity or even running water in their homes, women's domestic tasks such as laundry were hard, physical labor. Water had to be fetched and heated for washing and cooking. In addition, coal had to be carried, grates cleared, and fires lit each day. Without refrigerators and freezers to preserve food, and no convenient prepared meals, food had to be bought fresh and cooked each day.

Epitaph for a Tired Housewife

This traditional English rhyme in the style of a gravestone epitaph reflects the endless drudgery of women's housework before the introduction of labor-saving devices:

Here lies a poor woman who always was tired.
She lived in a house where help was not hired.
Her last words on earth were, "Dear friends, I am going
Where washing ain't done, nor sweeping nor sewing;
But everything there is exact to my wishes,
For where they don't eat there's no washing of dishes.
Don't mourn for me now, don't mourn for me never;
I'm going to do nothing for ever and ever."

Labor-saving devices

In the United States, Britain, and other Western countries, electricity began to be installed in the homes of the wealthy at the beginning of the century, and through the 1920s to 1940s for most people. Labor-saving devices, such as washing machines and vacuum cleaners, made housework easier, although only the rich could afford them at first.

Today in the Western world, most households have these machines, and they have reduced the hard labor involved in housework—but they have not necessarily reduced the amount of time spent on it, since standards of cleanliness have risen as a result. Many people now expect to wear clean clothes most days, which was not the case before washing machines were widely available. In **developing countries,** meanwhile, most women must still do chores such as laundry by hand.

The new domestic servants?

After World War I, only the very richest families continued to employ **domestic servants.** But toward the end of the twentieth century in the West, there was a rise in the number of people, usually women, employed to do domestic work in other people's homes. As more women went to work outside the home, ordinary middle-class families started to pay people to serve as housekeepers and nannies. As with domestic service in the early part of the century, this kind of work was often lonely and not well-paid. Thousands of women from developing countries, such as Malaysia, Thailand, and the Philippines, came as **migrant** workers to these jobs, sending their wages back home to support their families.

A house unkept

Women were, and are still at times, judged by their housekeeping standards. There were some early voices, though, that disagreed. In 1923, novelist Rose Macaulay told her readers:

Let the house go unkept. Let it go to the devil, and see what happens. At the worst, a house unkept cannot be so distressing as a life unlived.

These children go to daycare on a kibbutz (a cooperatively run community) in Israel. Many kibbutzim (kibbutz dwellers) organize shared cooking and child care to free women from the burden and isolation of domestic work.

Marriage, Motherhood, and Divorce

At the beginning of the twentieth century, marriage for most women meant shifting from their father's control to their husband's, with the possibilty of decades of pregnancies and child rearing. While many women considered their role as a mother very important, they argued that it did not receive the recognition and status it deserved. Throughout the twentieth century, women fought for access to **contraception** to enable them to plan when they started a family, and for more rights in marriage and **divorce.**

Birth control

Contraception, or **birth control,** allows people to plan if or when they have children. Before birth control, a married woman might have up to fifteen or more children, damaging her health and forcing her to spend most of her life caring for her family. Often poor families could not afford to care for so many children.

Margaret Sanger set up the first birth-control clinic in 1916 in New York. Lines formed outside. Sanger was arrested for breaking laws that restricted the distribution of contraceptives or information about them. But she won her case and went on to open 300 birth-control clinics. In Britain, despite protests from doctors and religious groups, Marie Stopes opened a birth-control clinic in London in 1921.

Margaret Sanger, American birth-control pioneer, appears with her supporters outside a court in New York.

In **developing countries** with poor health care, women continue to have large families because many children die from malnutrition and disease. With no **pensions** or **welfare system,** the children must provide for their parents in old age. Until parents can be sure that their children will survive, many do not want to use birth control. Also, some religions discourage the use of birth control as well.

Motherhood by the book

Throughout the twentieth century, women have been bombarded with advice from experts, often male, on how to raise children. Ideas have shifted from rigid discipline to the more affectionate and relaxed approach that is common today.

In the 1950s and 60s, mothers who worked outside the home were accused of harming their children, although working fathers were seldom criticized. By the end of the twentieth century, many women in the **West** were working full time, although in some countries part-time work had become a popular option, allowing mothers to earn money while still spending time with their children. Employment rights for working mothers have improved in the West, including maternity pay and the right to return to work after having children.

Women's property rights

Historically, when a woman married, everything she owned was transferred from her father's control to her husband's, because women were not allowed to own property, money, or goods. Gradually, through the late nineteenth and twentieth centuries, Western countries changed their laws to give women equal property rights. However, in many developing countries, husbands still control their wive's property.

Divorce

For centuries, divorce was illegal or difficult to obtain, even for women in the most unhappy, violent, or abusive marriages. Throughout the nineteenth and twentieth centuries, divorce has gradually been introduced in most countries around the world, despite disapproval from some religious leaders. And the divorce rate is rising. This is partly due to laws introduced in the 1960s that have made divorce easier for both men and women, and partly because of women's growing economic **independence.** Divorce courts try to divide a couple's money fairly, but many divorced women still end up with less money than before. This is because few women can earn as much as their husband, especially if they have responsibility for the children.

*In some Hindu wedding ceremonies, the bride's family is expected to pay a **dowry** to the husband's family. Some wives have been killed because their dowry is too small. Women in India are campaigning for an end to dowries and the violence they can bring.*

In some cultures divorce is legally available, but may not be a safe option for women in reality. In some Islamic countries, for example, there is great pressure on women to maintain the family honor. Women accused of bringing shame on the family by filing for divorce or by being unfaithful to their husbands can be severely punished.

Changes Since 1960

Women's rights came to the forefront again in the **West** in the 1960s, a time of fresh ideas and new freedom among young people. A new women's political movement called women's liberation questioned the role and status of women. Many changes shaped women's rights throughout the rest of the twentieth century.

Women's liberation movement

In the 1960s in the West, young women flocked to study at universities as their opportunities expanded. But women's job opportunities and earnings were still limited. Most women worked in low-paying clerical or service jobs. When they married, they were expected to stay at home and raise children.

In 1966, women in the United States, influenced by the **civil rights** movement of that time, set up the National Organization of Women (NOW). Women's liberation groups sprang up and their ideas spread quickly in many countries, rich and poor.

Like the **suffragists,** the women's liberation movement campaigned for equal pay and equal rights at work, but supporters were also fighting for equality in relationships. They believed that the personal relationships within an individual marriage or family were part of a wider political framework—a framework where men had more power than women.

A woman's right to choose

Women's liberation fought for a woman's right to decide for herself about her own life and her body, rather than her husband, family, employer, the government, or her religion deciding for her. Two other important developments of the time were the **contraceptive** pill and access to **abortion.**

Available in the 1960s, the contraceptive pill allowed women to have sex without fear of getting pregnant. At first, it was available to married women only. In Britain, the Marie Stopes

Demonstrators from the National Women's Liberation Movement protest at the Miss America Pageant in Atlantic City in 1968. As part of this protest, demonstrators crowned a sheep. Feminists found such beauty contests degrading and felt they encouraged men to judge only women's physical appearance.

Clinic held its first sessions for unmarried women in secret because many people disapproved. "The pill," as it is called, allowed women sexual freedom. But some feared that young women would come under pressure from men to have sex without being able to say no.

Abortion

Abortion, or termination of pregnancy, was illegal in most countries until the 1960s. Sometimes pregnant women were forced to seek out illegal abortions if they could not support a child because of poverty, health problems, or because of feelings of shame if they were young or unmarried. Many women died or became injured as a result of unsafe illegal abortions.

Feminists campaigned for the right to safe, legal abortion. A 1973 legal case in the United States, *Roe v. Wade*, gave women the right to abortion on restricted grounds. In the United States, abortion is still a complicated and controversial issue. For religious reasons, many people oppose abortion, sometimes violently, with attacks on doctors at abortion clinics.

Shaping the future

In the United States, feminists and other campaigners fought hard to change the constitution with the Equal Rights Amendment (ERA), which would have guaranteed equal treatment in all areas of life. Although it was accepted by Congress in 1972, the ERA never became law because several states refused to ratify it. The constitution remains without an Equal Rights Amendment. This was a major blow for women's rights in the United States.

Protestors attend an anti-abortion rally in London in 1975. The issue of abortion is split between those who think it is the woman's right to chose and those who feel that the rights of the unborn child need to be protected.

The women's liberation movement was fairly shortlived, and it remained a largely white and middle-class movement. Even so, many of the movement's aims were fulfilled, in the West at least. In Europe, legislation now outlaws unequal treatment of women. Young women in the West today expect freedom and equality as a matter of course.

Health Care and Medicine

The areas of health care and medicine developed rapidly in the twentieth century, bringing huge improvements in women's and men's health. However, many **developing countries** are still too poor for their people to benefit from medical advances, and women's health there is especially badly affected as a result.

New health services

In 1900, without adequate health care, many women suffered, especially poor women. Their health was weakened by frequent pregnancies. Many died during childbirth in dirty or dangerous surroundings, often without the help of a skilled doctor or nurse.

In recent years, many women's lives have been saved by preventative health care, such as screening for early symptoms of cancer. In much of Europe after World War II, national health services were set up or extended, offering free health care to all citizens. For millions of women, this meant that at last they could get proper care during pregnancy and childbirth. In the United States, however, where health care is based on private insurance, many poor women still do not get the medical care they need.

Women's psychological health

The last quarter of the twentieth century brought new concerns about women's psychological health in the **West.** Here, women are constantly bombarded with media images and advertising that show an ideal body shape—an ideal that is much thinner than most women's natural shape. The multi-million dollar dieting industry enforces this ideal.

These children in Nairobi, Kenya have been orphaned by the AIDS virus. They are protesting against drug companies who charge unaffordable prices for drugs that might have saved their parents' lives.

Pressures like this have led to a steep rise in anorexia and other eating disorders among girls and young women. Sometimes these disorders are so extreme that they lead to hospitalization and even death. At the same time, there is growing demand for expensive plastic surgery to change women's body shapes. Women undergo surgeries such as breast enlargement or reduction and facial alteration all in the quest for physical female "perfection." This is in stark contrast to some of the less developed countries of the world where the main concerns are hunger, malnutrition, and disease.

Women's health in developing countries

Many people in developing countries still live in poor conditions, often without sanitation or clean drinking water, and without access to doctors, nurses, or health care. In some very poor areas, such as parts of Bangladesh, as few as five percent of women giving birth are attended by a trained nurse or doctor, compared with around 98 percent in the West. A woman in Africa is 200 times more likely to die from a pregnancy-related complication than a woman in the West.

Women with HIV and AIDS

By the end of 2000, over 16 million women had HIV or AIDS, and over 80 percent of them lived in the developing world. In the more affluent West, drugs can be used to slow down the progress of the disease. People with AIDS there can now expect to live for many years. But in less wealthy parts of the world, governments cannot afford the drugs' high prices, so people with AIDS cannot live as long.

Reproductive technology

Since the 1970s, reproductive technology has used new scientific methods to overcome **infertility,** bringing great joy to some women who would otherwise have been unable to have babies. However, treatment is very expensive and often unsuccessful, and many insurance companies will not pay for it.

Reproductive technology is developing very quickly, and it raises many complex issues. Now that tests can show the sex of an embryo in the womb, female embryos are sometimes **aborted** because parents want a son instead. In addition, some parents leave their baby girls to die because they want a boy. This has led to a serious population imbalance in countries such as Pakistan and China, where there are tens of millions of "missing females."

*Louise Brown, the world's first test-tube baby, was born in 1978. She was conceived by **in vitro fertilization.** Here her parents talk on television about the events leading up to her birth.*

27

Women and Work 1900–1939

At the beginning of the twentieth century, while many wealthy women stayed at home, working-class women worked long hours for low pay. Women were excluded from many jobs by their limited education or by employers' expectations. For instance, very few women were able to train and work as doctors or other professionals. World War I, however, brought major changes to women's work.

Women as workers

In 1900, working-class women worked to help make ends meet for their families, often in difficult and hazardous jobs. They were paid less than men, and they could rarely join **trade unions,** which fought for better rights and pay. In cities, some women worked in **sweatshops,** places that demanded a lot of hard work for the very lowest pay. In rural and coastal areas, women worked in the fields or in the fishing industry. Millions more women toiled for hours every day as **domestic servants.**

Women in World War I

In 1914, war broke out and governments all over the world began to encourage women to take over the jobs left empty by men who had gone to fight. Women worked as bus drivers, in police forces, and in weapon-making factories. By 1917, there were over 700,000 women in Germany working in heavy industry—six times as many as there were in 1913.

These German window cleaners are on their way to work in 1905. Working-class women did many types of heavy work.

War work, for many women, meant twelve-hour shifts, seven days a week—and they were still paid far less than the men who had been doing the same jobs. But, old prejudices were challenged as women coped well with their new jobs.

Some women traveled to where the fighting was taking place to serve as nurses and ambulance drivers. A few took on daring roles as spies and resistance fighters behind enemy lines, including Edith Cavell, a British nurse who helped prisoners escape, and a Dutch dancer known as Mata Hari who worked as a German spy.

After the War

Women, especially those who were married, were expected to leave their new jobs for the soldiers returning from the war. But the world was changing. Many women were reluctant to give up their newfound **independence,** and were prepared to explore new types of work to earn a living. Domestic service was growing increasingly unpopular. All over the United States and Europe, women took jobs in factories, where new mass-production methods were used to make all kinds of goods, from cars to shoes to typewriters. Office and retail work provided a better future for many aspiring young women from the middle classes.

Depression and the New Deal

In 1929, the **Great Depression** rippled around the world. Unemployment soared, reaching 30 percent of the workforce in some countries. Many women were poor and hungry, especially those who needed to earn money to support their families.
In the United States, President Roosevelt set up the New Deal, which created public service jobs building dams and other huge projects to get people back to work. But only a few plans for women were set up.

Rather than starve in the drought-ridden Dust Bowl states during the 1930s, women and their families abandoned their farms and traveled to California in search of work. Photographer Dorothea Lange, who took this picture, documented their desperate plight.

Paid holidays

Most workers did not get paid holidays until the 1930s. A French woman remembers:
You have no idea what a tremendous joy it was to get paid holidays. The whole of Paris, all the workshops, all the factories, everywhere people went crazy.

The Dust Bowl

For rural women on small farms all around the world, life was grueling and often lonely. They lived, worked, and raised families in difficult conditions, often in homes without electricity or toilets. In the 1930s, in the Great Plains states, massive dust storms whipped away the thin topsoil, loosened by lack of rain and decades of farming. On thousands of small family farms, it was impossible to grow food or cotton crops and families starved.

Women's Service in World War II

Women played an even more active role in World War II than they had in World War I. Once again, governments needed women to take over men's jobs at home. This time, war work brought important changes in women's employment, including part-time work and demands for equal pay.

Women in military service

Although some senior officers disapproved in both the United States and Britain, women's units were set up in many of the armed forces. Women pilots were eventually allowed to fly military planes. They were put to work taking planes to where they were needed. Women also trained for technical tasks, such as guiding pilots by radio, and operating radar devices and anti-aircraft searchlights. General Eisenhower, supreme commander in the Allied invasion of Germany and future president, was a strong supporter of women in active roles behind the lines.

Women pilots of the British Air Transport Auxiliary Service, piloted planes from factories to airports during World War II.

A war-work organizer remembers:

I remember three girls from Bootle [Lancashire, England]. They were marvelous. They became the most efficient tractor drivers . . . I can't think of anything they couldn't do.

War work at home

All across Europe, women worked in munitions factories to support their country's war effort. In Britain in 1941, women under 40 were **conscripted** for war work in the factories, fields, or in other essential jobs. In the United States there was no conscription, but **propaganda** campaigns encouraged women to support the war effort.

A lasting image from this era is "Rosie the Riveter," painted by Norman Rockwell, and featured on the front cover of the *Saturday Evening Post,* a popular magazine of the time. Rosie looked strong and capable of anything. Such propaganda was successful in persuading women to train as welders, electricians, and for other labor-intensive jobs.

Equal rights at work?

But even in war work, sexual and racial **discrimination** were widespread. Some male supervisors were reluctant to believe that women could do the work as well as men, although they were soon proven wrong. Women were still paid less than men for the same jobs. African-American women were often directed to badly paid jobs, for instance, kitchen work, until protest marches got them into higher paid manufacturing work. Many more women joined **trade unions** to demand equal pay.

This magazine cover features Rosie the Riveter, painted by Norman Rockwell. Propaganda like this encouraged American women to lend their muscle to the war effort.

There were other changes, too. Part-time work was introduced to fit around women's responsibilities at home. And more women worked as dentists, lawyers, and architects. Women photographers, like Margaret Bourke-White and Lee Miller, and journalists such as Martha Gellhorn and Iris Morley, recorded the horrors of war. Iris Morley was one of the first correspondents to send news of the Nazi concentration camps in 1945.

Child care for women war workers

British propaganda posters were published to encourage people to look after war workers' children:
If you can't go to the factory, help the neighbour who can.
Caring for war workers' children is a national service.
Arrange now with a neighbour to look after her children when she goes to her war work.

Child care

When women's labor was needed for the war effort, many governments set up daycare centers to look after children, allowing mothers to go out to work. However, in the U.S., most working mothers still had to make their own arrangements for child care while they worked.

Women's Work in the Post-War Era

By the end of World War II in 1945, Europe was devastated. With millions of men killed or missing, it was often the women who started rebuilding. From the late 1950s onward, the **West** enjoyed decades of confidence and prosperity. But there were hard times for women in other parts of the world.

Back to the kitchen

When peace came, just as after World War I, women in the West were expected to leave their jobs for the returning men. Having experienced a few years of financial **independence,** many women found this disappointing and frustrating.

The United States had grown stronger through the war, while Europe and Japan worked hard to rebuild shattered industries. By the mid-1950s, living standards in the West and Japan had risen to higher levels than before the war. Peace and optimism brought a baby boom, with families having children in increasing numbers. But although they had proven their worth in the workplace, women, and especially mothers, were encouraged to stay at home. Their real work was seen as bringing up the children and keeping a spotless home. Middle-class women who did work were mainly confined to traditionally female jobs, such as teaching, nursing, or secretarial work. Working-class women often worked shifts in factories that fit around child care responsibilities, or they worked in kitchens or did cleaning work.

These women are resurfacing roads in Moscow, a job usually seen in the West as men's work.

Trade union struggles

Women were still paid less than men for doing the same work. In 1965, women's earnings in the United States were still only 60 percent of men's earnings. Many women, including badly paid African-American, Asian, and Hispanic women, joined **trade unions** to fight against **discrimination** at work. Strikes by women, such as those by health workers in New York, showed that their work was as important as men's. Gradually, these struggles brought about some improvement in women's rights at work.

Sexual harassment flourished in the male culture of many workplaces, restricting women's careers and making their working lives

uncomfortable. In the 1980s, the United States issued regulations that made sexual harassment on the job a form of discrimination. The Supreme Court ruled it to be illegal in 1986. Today, many employers enforce strict policies on sexual harrassment to keep the workplace safe for all employees.

British workers went on strike for better rights at work in the 1970s. Many black and Asian women took their struggle for equal rights through the trade unions.

Women in the Communist world

In the Soviet Union so many men had been killed in World War II that many women remained unmarried or brought up children on their own. Western ideas about traditional male and female roles did not apply in the **Communist** world, where women worked as engineers, doctors, machinists, and laborers. Women were expected to work long hours in factories on the same terms as men.

However, many Communist economies failed to provide the ordinary goods that would improve women's day-to-day lives. There were frequent food shortages, and women had to wait in line at markets every day to buy enough to feed their families.

Women's work in developing countries

Women in **developing countries** were badly affected by changes during this time. In the 1960s and 70s, wealthy nations sent aid in the form of loans to help developing countries build up their industry. But as interest rates rose, the cost of paying back the loans rose steeply. Many poor countries were forced to cut services such as health care and education. This hit women especially hard, as they needed medical care during pregnancy and were often responsible for bringing up their children. Unemployment, poverty, and hunger grew rapidly.

Women's Work at the End of the Century

"Equal pay for equal work," a central plank of the women's liberation movement of the 1970s, has not yet been achieved everywhere. But by the end of the twentieth century, women were able to choose a far wider range of jobs, including manual and professional roles, which had always been seen as men's work.

Equal pay?

By 2000, women's earnings in the United States were hovering at around 75 percent, just three-quarters the rate of men's earnings. But this figure masked wide variations; for instance, Hispanic women in the U.S. earned just 48 cents for every dollar earned by a man.

Child care for working mothers

While women without children were finding more and more work opportunities opening up to them at the end of the century, women with children still faced many barriers. Employers were often reluctant to hire women with children, fearing a clash in the responsibilities of work and family. Reliable and affordable child care for those who wanted to return to work was the only solution to this problem.

Scandinavia led the way, providing plenty of high-quality child care for mothers who went to work. But in other countries, child care was expensive and in short supply. Many women are still forced to rely on uncertain arrangements with relatives, friends, and neighbors to look after their children after school and during vacations.

An American female soldier takes a break during training exercises in Saudi Arabia.

Women in traditionally male jobs

Women fought for the right to work in many fields that had been traditionally reserved for men. For example, in 1992, the Church of England began to ordain women priests, following more progressive U.S. and British churches and synagogues, which had allowed women priests and rabbis since the 1970s. By the end of the twentieth century, women could also serve as soldiers in the front line along with men in many countries.

Throughout the twentieth century, women gradually overcame male resistance to work as scientists. Even then, they often had to fight for recognition, as male colleagues sometimes took credit for their work.

Globalization

In the 1980s and 90s, **multinational corporations** started to move their manufacturing from the **West** to factories in Asia and Latin America. There they could pay workers (often women) much lower wages than they could in the West. This is part of a process called **globalization.** In countries such as China, Malaysia, and Mexico, young women worked in factories, manufacturing electronic equipment, textiles, and footwear. Many worked up to eighteen hours a day in conditions that were often harmful to their health. Fortunately, **trade unions** and other organizations put pressure on these corporations to improve working conditions in their factories. However, there is still progress to be made.

As a result of globalization, many factories closed down across the United States and Europe. Millions of jobs were lost. In many cities, new work patterns emerged. Part-time jobs in service industries such as foodservice, mainly filled by women, replaced men's jobs in manufacturing.

This woman is working in an electronics factory in China in 1987. As part of the globalization process, large multinational corporations have moved their factories to countries where pay and working conditions are lower than in the West.

Women in business

Women found it more difficult than men to set up their own businesses because money lenders were often sceptical about whether women had the necessary skills to be business owners. One example is Anita Roddick. She had great difficulty persuading any bank to lend her money to start opening shops to sell her goods. Despite this, her international business, The Body Shop, has become very successful. Other successful business women include fashion designer Donna Karan and entertainer and entrepreneur Oprah Winfrey, who has gone on to manage her own production company.

Entertainment, Media, and the Arts

Throughout history, women have worked as actors, singers, and entertainers, although they have had to fight for equal pay. But in many other art forms, women have had to challenge prejudice to be taken seriously and to get funding for their work. Often they have struggled to carve out time from their domestic responsibilities for their art. Women have fought for a more influential role in the new media forms that developed throughout the twentieth century, from radio and cinema to television and information technology.

Craft or art?

Women's traditional creative skills in needlework have been downgraded as craft, rather than as higher-status art. Even at the radical German Bauhaus college of architecture and design, set up in 1919, women were expected to work only in textiles. They had to fight to take part in other art forms, such as painting or architecture.

Women in film, theater, and television

In the first half of the twentieth century, going to the movies was hugely popular. A study in 1937 found some women and girls went twelve times a week. Glamorous female Hollywood filmstars were models of feminine style, and often grew very rich. However, women who wanted to direct their own films had to struggle to raise funds, and very few succeeded in becoming filmmakers. In the theater, the situation was better and more women directors found success there.

The single most important mass medium of the twentieth century was television, and the number of women journalists and directors grew toward the end of the century. Although news agendas were still largely dictated by male interests, some women journalists became leaders in the field and reported from war zones around the world. Individual women also had an immense impact on culture through television. For instance, Oprah Winfrey shaped the reading habits of millions with her monthly television bookclub.

Oprah Winfrey, successful actress, talk show host, and business woman, interviewed presidential candidate Al Gore on her television program in September 2000.

Women writers

Historically, women writers have had an uphill battle to get their work published and often they've had to resort to adopting a male pen name in order to do so. As the twentieth century progressed, more and more women's writing found its way into print. Particularly from the 1970s onward, women's writing flourished, promoted by both **feminist** and mainstream publishers. Women such as Toni Morrison and Maya Angelou wrote from a female African-American perspective, and their books won much popular acclaim.

Evelyn Glennie is a world renowned percussionist with a hearing disability. Most orchestras have abandoned their men-only traditions, employing women musicians on equal terms. One exception is the Vienna Philharmonic Orchestra, which still bans women.

Women musicians

Women musicians have often struggled to make a living from their work. In the segregated southern states, African-American musicians were rarely allowed to perform for white audiences. In the 1920s, African-American jazz singer Josephine Baker worked instead in more liberal France, where she became a star. In the 1960s, African-American women's musical groups such as the Supremes achieved great popularity, but often their recording contracts meant that they kept little of the money their success earned. By the end of the twentieth century this situation had changed and there are now many examples of successful women earning large fortunes through popular music.

Female composers, like other female artists, have had to struggle to get their work in front of an audience. American composer Ruth Schonthal reflected on the experience of women artists in many fields when she said, "It has been a tremendous struggle to find time and energy to compose." Without the recognition and funding that support many male composers, she earned her living by teaching and playing in clubs.

Funny women

Female comedians were a relative rarity until late in the twentieth century—women were expected to be beautiful, but not funny. Singer and comic Bette Midler was an exception, starring in performances and movies from the late 1960s on. In the 1980s, however, more and more women comedians started to break into television sitcoms and stand-up comedy.

Fashion Statements

Women's clothing has been an indicator of sexual politics, with fashion items such as corsets and high heels often cramping women's freedom of movement. From long skirts in 1900 to power suits in 2000, sweeping changes in **Western** women's fashions have mirrored some of the changes in women's lives.

Health and wealth

In 1900, women wore full-length skirts for modesty, with tightly laced corsets to cinch their waists, often restricting their breathing and damaging their health. Wealthy women displayed their riches by wearing elaborate, opulent gowns. Meanwhile, poor women might own only one dress, which would be worn and mended again and again.

Coco Chanel (left), a French fashion designer, designed stylish, loose-fitting clothing made of soft, comfortable fabric. Many women welcomed these relaxed new fashions.

New Woman, new look

Fashion began to change early in the twentieth century, as so-called "New Women" began to challenge some of the traditional expectations of how women should dress. Some started wearing slacks, which allowed them more freedom of movement. Skirt hemlines rose, though not yet above the knee.

After World War I, women started to abandon their corsets and some of the old, restrictive fashions. Coco Chanel, a French designer working in Paris, designed loose-fitting fashions made of soft, comfortable fabrics. Flappers, fashionable young women of the 1920s, danced in revealing dresses that seemed shocking at the time.

Wartime concerns

During both world wars, new clothes were a rare luxury. In some countries, fabric was rationed along with food and furniture. Governments encouraged fashions that required less fabric—for instance, shorter, more narrow skirts. Then, when peace came, women enjoyed new and more relaxed fashions again.

The shock of the young

Young women's fashions in the second half of the twentieth century often seemed outrageous to older generations. Women's clothes in the 1960s reflected the sexual freedom of the times. Hemlines rose and rose until the mini skirt couldn't get any shorter. **Androgynous** styles, suitable for both sexes, reduced the difference between women's and men's clothing among youth in the 1960s, and again in the late 1970s when punk rock spread from Britain around the world. Young punk rockers rejected their parents' values, dressing in ripped black clothing held together with safety pins. Women and men alike wore bold makeup and spiky hairstyles supported by hairspray and styling gel.

East, west, best dressed?

Western designers have often borrowed fashion ideas from around the world, from Indian prints to African textiles. But Western fashions influenced people in other cultures, too, often weakening distinctive local styles and traditions.

"No Logo"

Throughout the developed world, fashion has been dominated by heavily-advertised brands. Branded clothing and shoes are sold at very high prices, despite being cheaply manufactured in **developing countries** by poorly paid workers—mainly women and children. This increases the manufacturers' profits.

Naomi Klein, a young Canadian woman, is one of the leaders of the "No Logo" movement. This movement protests against such profiteering, which cheats both the workers and the consumers. Supporters of this movement work for better working conditions for people making clothes, shoes, and other goods.

Clothing at school

Many girls are forced to wear a skirt as part of their school uniform. Some girls have argued that this **discriminates** against them because it is impractical and uncomfortable in cold weather. Individual girls have challenged school rules, taking their cases to court. Recent court rulings have decided that it is unfair for schools to impose different rules for girls and boys.

This French girl is protesting a ban on wearing the Islamic veil at school. In France it is argued that schools should be **secular,** not religious, establishments. Some Islamic girls there are forced to choose between their faith and their education.

Women in Sports

In the early 1900s, women were expected to take part only in "ladylike" sports. Athleticism and competition were thought to be unhealthy for women. Throughout the twentieth century, women fought to take part in all sports, and to receive equal rewards for winning.

"Ladies sports"

Traditional ladies' sports were restricted to tennis, badminton, croquet, and golf, together with dancing, horseback riding, and skating. In women's long, restrictive clothing, most other sports were impractical. In addition, there was concern that too much physical exercise might damage women's health and their ability to have children.

New freedoms

The 1920s saw a break away from these concerns. Isadora Duncan's free-expression dancing increased the popularity of exercise through movement to music. Ballet became increasingly popular, too, and many dance schools opened.

In 1994, Liv Arnesen of Sweden became the first woman to ski alone to the South Pole.

In 1926, nineteen-year-old Gertrude Ederle broke both male and female records when she swam the English Channel in just fourteen and a half hours, challenging sceptics who thought that women could not compete athletically with men. Other 1920s record breakers included golfer Glenn Collate, and Floret McCrutcheon, who defeated the reigning male champion Jimmy Smith, in 1927 in bowling. Commercial organizers began to see that women could attract large crowds at sporting events.

The Olympic Games

Women were barred from the modern Olympic Games until 1920, when they were allowed to compete in a very limited range of sports. In reaction to this, the Women's Olympic Games were held between 1922 and 1934, and attracted competitors and spectators from all over the world. Since then, the proportion of women taking part in the Olympics has risen steadily, reaching 38 percent in 2000. Some national teams, including Norway and China, have been made up of over 50 percent women athletes.

Nontraditional sports

In the 1970s, women began to take up traditionally male sports. For instance, by 1976 there were 10,000 women weightlifters in the United States. In 1974, ten-year-old Frances Pescatore was not allowed to play baseball in a Little League team in New Jersey. She challenged this **discrimination,** and won the right to play along with the boys.

In the United States, the Women's National Basketball Association (WNBA) kicked off its first season in 1997, generating much excitement among female athletes and the general public alike. Girls' and women's soccer teams are now popular all over the world, and women's cricket tournaments are very popular in cricketing countries. Today women compete in sports such as shot putting, wrestling, and even boxing.

Britain's Tanni Grey-Thompson competes at the Paralympic Games, which take place just after the Olympic Games. There is increasing worldwide interest, sponsorship, and television coverage of the Paralympic Games.

Equal prize money

Sports competition organizers had always paid women less prize money than men. In 1970, top women tennis players including Billie Jean King, Rosemary Casals, and Ann Jones protested this by refusing to play. The organizers soon had to give in. Women drew in massive audiences, and there was no justification for smaller prizes. One commentator conceded that these women had proven their worth "game, set, and match." But this battle has had to be fought by women again and again in many sports.

Women's Rights into the 21st Century

By the end of the twentieth century, women had gained many more rights than their great-grandmothers had a hundred years earlier. But there is still much work to be done to win equal rights for all the world's women in the 21st century and beyond.

Girls and women succeeding

Girls are achieving in school, and, in the **West** at least, women go on to college in similar numbers to men. At work, too, women are developing their careers and moving into senior positions. Equal pay for equal work is accepted in principle, and many countries now have maternity benefits to make sure that women can take time off to have a family and then resume their careers.

However, the proportion of women in very top jobs, such as managing director and CEO, is still small. Many women reach an invisible barrier, known as the glass ceiling, that prevents them from achieving these kinds of senior positions. Sex **segregation** is still common in the workplace, with women concentrated in lower-paid fields such as foodservice and child care.

The double burden

In many couples where both partners work full-time, women find that they are still doing most or all of the shopping, cooking, and cleaning. This is known as the "double burden." Women also spend more time than men caring for their children and elderly relatives. Studies have shown that these tasks leave women with less leisure time than men.

This woman has purchased a rickshaw with a loan from the Grameen Bank in Bangladesh. This bank lends small amounts of money to women so that they can start businesses, often bringing their families out of generations of poverty.

Women and poverty

In the West, **welfare systems** have helped lessen hunger and malnutrition. But according to the **United Nations,** in 1995 about a quarter of the world's population was still living in extreme poverty in **developing countries,** on an income of less than one dollar each day. Of these, nearly three-quarters were women and girls, who get less education and training to gain the skills needed to get out of poverty.

Many developing countries were also burdened with the problem of repaying the interest on loans made to them by more wealthy nations. This often resulted in them having to take money away from welfare, health, and education services. Some people argue that the rich West should no longer demand these enormous interest payments. Some governments in the West have made a start on this process. In 1999, they promised to cancel debts totalling $100 billion, although less than $12 billion had actually been written off by the end of the century.

Gains and losses

Women's campaigns achieved improved rights in many countries around the world. But in some areas, women's rights are decreasing. In Afghanistan and other countries with **fundamentalist** regimes, women are not allowed to study, work, or even drive. Many Islamic women have argued that true Islam should not oppress women, and are trying to improve women's rights within the faith.

Perhaps the greatest shift throughout the twentieth century was in women's, and men's, expectations. By the end of the century, whether or not they called themselves **feminists,** most women in the West expected equal rights in all areas of life. However, for millions of women around the world, the struggle for equal rights—as well as for basic human needs such as food, shelter, education, and health care—continues into the 21st century.

*Since the fall of **Communism** in the late 1980s, life has become harder for many women in Eastern Europe. Some take on hazardous work to support themselves and their families. The woman pictured above is handling coils of asbestos, which is an extremely toxic material.*

Still a long way to go...

An official United Nations report in 1980 stated: "Although women are fifty percent of the world's adult population, they comprise one third of the official labor force, perform nearly two thirds of all working hours, receive only one tenth of world income, and own less than one percent of world property."

Timeline

1902	Women in Australia gain the right to vote, nine years after women in New Zealand
1900– 1914	**Suffragists** campaign for women's votes in the United States, Britain, and around the world
1903	British suffragists form the Women's Social and Political Union to fight for women's votes
1914	Outbreak of World War I
1915	Women's International League for Peace and Freedom formed at peace conference at The Hague
1916	Margaret Sanger opens the first **birth-control** clinic in the United States
1917	Russian Revolution: women's rights improve in the new Soviet Union
1918	End of World War I
	British women over the age of 30 gain the right to vote
1920	Women in the United States gain the right to vote
	Women first allowed to compete in the Olympic Games
1928	All women gain the right to vote in Britain at the same age as men (21)
1939	Outbreak of World War II
1941	**Conscription** for war work introduced for British women
1945	End of World War II
	Women in France gain the right to vote
1948	Universal Declaration of **Human Rights** adopted by the **United Nations**
1949	**Communist** Party takes control of China; women's rights improve
1955– 1967	Women active in the U.S. **civil rights** movement, campaigning for equal rights for people of all races
1960	Sirimavo Bandaranaika of Sri Lanka is the first woman to be elected prime minister
	The **contraceptive** pill becomes available
1965	Civil Rights Act ends **segregation** in the United States
1966	The National Organization for Women formed in the United States
	The women's liberation movement flourishes
1967	**Abortion** becomes legal under certain conditions in Britain
1971	Women in Switzerland gain the right to vote
1972	Equal Rights Amendment adopted by U.S. Congress, although it is never ratified
1973	*Roe v. Wade* allows abortion in United States under very limited circumstances
1975	United Nations women's conference launches the UN Decade for Women
1979	Convention on Elimination of All Forms of **Discrimination** Against Women (CEDAW) adopted by the United Nations
	Some governments, including the United States, refuse to sign
	Margaret Thatcher elected prime minister of Britain
1980	Petra Kelly becomes chairperson of the Green Party in Germany, the first woman to head a German political party
1980s	Women campaign against nuclear weapons stationed in Europe, Australia, and North America
1984	Arson and bomb attacks on U.S. abortion clinics rise steeply
1989	Fall of Communism begins in the Soviet Union and Eastern Europe; life becomes harder for many women
1990	Aung San Suu Kyi elected as leader of Burma, although she is not allowed to govern
1994	Women ordained as Anglican priests in the Church of England
1995	United Nations women's conference in Beijing: Global Platform for Action on women's rights
1996	The Taliban, Islamic **fundamentalists,** gradually take control in Afghanistan, undermining women's rights
1997	Labour government elected to power in Britain with the highest proportion of women in British history
	Mary Robinson, former president of Ireland, becomes the UN High Commissioner for Human Rights
	Madeleine Albright becomes U.S. secretary of state

Further Reading

Blackman, Cally. *20th Century Fashion: The 20s & 30s: Flappers & Vamps.* Milwaukee: Gareth Stevens, 1999.

Collins, Eileen and Amy Nathan. *Yankee Doodle Gals: Women Pilots of World War II.* Washington D.C.: National Geographic, 2001.

Colman, Penny. *Rosie the Riveter: Women Working on the Home Front in World War II.* New York: Random House, 1995.

Gourley, Catherine. *Good Girl Work: Factories, Sweatshops, and How Women Changed Their Role in the American Workforce.* Brookfield, Conn.: Millbrook Press, 1999.

Harvey, Miles. *Women's Voting Rights: Story of the 19th Amendment.* Danbury, Conn.: Children's Press, 1996.

Hurley, Jennifer. *Great Speeches in History: Women's Rights.* Farmington Hills, Mich.: Greenhaven Press, 2001.

MacDonald, Fiona. *Women in a Changing World, 1945–2000.* New York: Peter Bedrick Books, 2000.

MacDonald, Fiona. *Women in Peace & War, 1900–1945.* New York: Peter Bedrick Books, 2000.

Mee, Sue. *20th Century Fashion: 1900–1920: Linen & Lace.* Milwaukee: Gareth Stevens, 1999.

Powe-Temperly, Kitty. *20th Century Fashion: The 60s: Mods & Hippies.* Milwaukee: Gareth Stevens, 1999.

Rust-Nash, Carol. *The Fight for Women's Right to Vote in American History.* Berkeley Heights, NJ: Enslow Publishers, 1998.

Stearman, Kaye and Nikki Vander Gaag. *Gender Issues.* New York: Raintree Steck-Vaughn, 1996.

Williams, Mary. *Working Women.* Farmington Hills, Mich.: Greenhaven Press, 1997.

Glossary

abortion ending a pregnancy, usually in the first few months

androgynous not defined by gender. In fashion, clothing that can be worn by both men and women is androgynous.

apartheid system in South Africa in which blacks and other non-whites were kept apart from whites and deprived of civil rights and basic freedoms such as the right to vote, to travel freely, and to choose where to live. The apartheid system was ended in 1994.

birth control see *contraception*

boycott refusal to take part in an activity as a form of protest

civil rights rights of a citizen to personal freedom, including the right to vote, and sexual and racial equality

Cold War state of hostility between the United States and its allies and the Soviet Union and its allies during the 1950s and 60s

colony area of land that is ruled by another country

Communism political and economic system in which the government owns the means of production, such as factories and farms, and controls the production and distribution of goods

conscription mandatory enrollment for military or other service; also called the draft

contraception birth control, such as a condom or pill, that prevents pregnancy and allows people to choose whether or when to have children

developing country country, usually in the southern hemisphere, that has not yet developed its full economic or industrial potential

discrimination treatment of people differently (usually worse), based on their sex, race, or for other reasons

divorce ending a marriage

domestic service working as a servant in someone else's, usually a wealthy person's, home

domestic violence violence at home; usually, but not always, male violence against a woman

dowry money or goods paid by the bride's family to the husband's family when a marriage takes place

felling cutting down trees

feminism movement supporting women's rights and equality. The modern feminist movement began toward the end of the nineteenth century, alongside the women's suffrage movement.

fundamentalist abiding by the strict rules and traditions of a particular religion

globalization process of the flow of goods, services, money, people, and information becoming widespread across national borders

Great Depression period of worldwide unemployment and poverty starting in 1929 and continuing through the 1930s

house arrest being forced against one's will to remain at home

human rights rights of every man, woman, and child to live free from fear of persecution, discrimination, injustice, and violence

independence self-rule of a country; also, being able to look after oneself

indigenous people original inhabitants of a region

infertility inability to have children

in vitro fertilization medical process in which an egg is fertilized outside the body and then implanted in the mother

literacy ability to read and write

mangle a device that dries laundry by passing it through rollers

migrant someone who travels from one area or country to another, usually in search of seasonal work

multinational corporation large business that is run for profit, and which trades and manufactures goods in many countries

pension payment made by a government or other organization to someone who has retired from work due to age, illness, or disability

propaganda publicity that is used to sway opinions and make people believe in something

refugee someone who flees their homeland to escape persecution

revolution dramatic change; also refers to the overthrow of a ruler or government by a mass action of the people

secular not having to do with spiritual or religious matters

segregation separateness or the act of being kept apart

suffrage right to vote in elections

suffragette or **suffragist** someone who supports the right to vote

superpower one of the most powerful nations in the world

sweatshop factory with poor working conditions where people work in an overcrowded and often unhealthy environment for very low pay

trade union organization of workers whose goal is to ensure fair wages and working conditions

United Nations (UN) international organization of governments of independent states. The UN was set up in 1945 after World War II and aims to promote understanding and peace between nations of the world.

welfare system system set up by a government to ensure education, health care, and enough money to live on for all citizens

West; Western country non-geographical term for one of the wealthy, industrialized countries of western and northern Europe, North America, Australia, and New Zealand

Index